T0204636

HUM

ALSO BY ANN LAUTERBACH

If in Time: Selected Poems 1975–2000

On a Stair

And for Example

Clamor

Before Recollection

Many Times, But Then

The Night Sky: Writings on the Poetics of Experience

BOOKS WITH ARTISTS

Thripsis
(with Joe Brainard)

A Clown, Some Colors, A Doll, Her Stories,
A Song, A Moonlit Cove
(with Ellen Phelan)

How Things Bear Their Telling
(with Lucio Pozzi)

Greeks
(with Jan Groover and Bruce Boice)

Sacred Weather
(with Louisa Chase)

HUM

ANN LAUTERBACH

PENGUIN POETS

PENGUIN BOOKS

Published by the Penguin Group
Penguin Group (USA) Inc., 375 Hudson Street, New York, New York 10014 U.S.A.
Penguin Group (Canada), 10 Alcorn Avenue, Toronto, Ontario, Canada M4V 3B2
(a division of Pearson Penguin Canada Inc.)
Penguin Books Ltd, 80 Strand, London WC2R 0RL, England
Penguin Ireland, 25 St Stephen's Green, Dublin 2, Ireland (a division of Penguin Books Ltd)
Penguin Group (Australia), 250 Camberwell Road, Camberwell, Victoria 3124, Australia
(a division of Pearson Australia Group Pty Ltd)
Penguin Books India Pvt Ltd, 11 Community Centre, Panchsheel Park,
New Delhi - 110 017, India
Penguin Group (NZ), cnr Airborne and Rosedale Roads, Albany, Auckland 1310, New Zealand
(a division of Pearson New Zealand Ltd)
Penguin Books (South Africa) (Pty) Ltd, 24 Sturdee Avenue, Rosebank,
Johannesburg 2196, South Africa

Penguin Books Ltd, Registered Offices:
80 Strand, London WC2R 0RL, England

First published in Penguin Books 2005

3   5   7   9   10   8   6   4   2

Page xi constitutes an extension of this copyright page.

LIBRARY OF CONGRESS CATALOGING-IN-PUBLICATION DATA
Lauterbach, Ann, 1942–
Hum / Ann Lauterbach.
p. cm.
ISBN 0-14-303496-0
I. Title.
PS3562.A844H86 2005
811'.54—dc22   2004058740

Printed in the United States of America
Set in Adobe Garamond with Shelley Andante Script
Designed by Jennifer Daddio

for Tom

ACKNOWLEDGMENTS

Some of these poems appeared, often in earlier drafts, in the following journals; I thank their editors: *Avec, The Bard Papers, Conjunctions, Court Green, Fence, Five Fingers Review, No: A Journal of the Arts; 26: A Journal of Poetry and Poetics.*

"Bookmark, Horizon" first appeared in *A Convergence of Birds, Original Fiction and Poetry Inspired by the Work of Joseph Cornell*, edited by Jonathan Safran Foer (New York, Distributed Art Publishers, Inc., 2001). "Detail 858-6 (Gerhard Richter)" was published in *Richter 858 Eight Abstract Pictures*, edited by David Breskin (San Francisco, The Shifting Foundation, SF MOMA; distributed by D.A.P.). "After Mahler" was published in *The Best American Poetry 2004*, edited by Lyn Hejinian (New York, Scribners).

For the score to Mahler's *Kindertotenlieder*, used on the jacket, thanks to Karen Garthe.

Thanks also to my marvelous agent, Lourdes Lopez, and to my editor at Penguin, Paul Slovak, for his continued support of this work.

What, art mad? A man may see how this world goes
with no eyes. Look with thine ears.
—SHAKESPEARE, KING LEAR, IV.6

If you listen with your ear, it is hard to understand.
If you hear with your eye, you are intimate at last.
—WU-MEN KUAN

CONTENTS

One

AFTER MAHLER

TENT

Maybe it will fall away.
Maybe what is interesting will also be beautiful
although that is—
               that is:
not to look out or at, but into.
Come closer, so close
what you see can be seen as hindsight.
The form seems too simple.
The form seems an error of judgment.
As if one had jumped across a boundary
to find the missing gift, left
in the brute junk of wandering gangs.
This is another way of speaking about intention,
about the theater of gathering.

LUCK

The day, you see? Huge, like Texas.
I saw a hawk today the birds froze.
Today I saw a hawk the small birds were still.
A hawk on a branch tail and shoulders
straight, a *soldier* is what I thought,
its small head moved in all directions
excellent robot I thought.
The small birds were still
as if without life
to escape the eye of the hawk.

The day, you see? Huge,
like Texas, or Bach,
Bach never still,
it is the nature of Bach not to stay still
to move in the orders of Bach
sometimes they seem limitless
as if out of the earth's orbit
or to come to the limits of earth
and then to go on
up over down
so that day can no longer be seen.
The boys in the water froze.
The thing over Texas broke up.

ETYMOLOGY

You will have been glad
iconography sweetly daunted   what is the *ab*
in abjection? Keith wondered.
We sought no rule. The piano was, after all, a man.
And she reached her slender arms into it, made it
slur its edges into sonic attenuation.
And the man rammed his throat onto his
long instrument, its
noise gathered and broke from.
                         At school, those who
had some notion of history
quoted it, as if it were a thing away,
others simply traversed its wake
into sampling and presence
as if the dead president
were finally of no account
other than his horse and carnage.
History failed to come forth, it spat back
trivia and made a form.
                         So these are the famous shoes
and this the painted mountain
and these are the vernacular ghosts
strutting their tunes into the storm,
its violent indifference.
                         The catbird walked along the grass
and took bugs back to the nest.
She seemed almost friendly in her indifference.

But the subject, its identity, proclaimed
nothing so much as similarity, a field
halted at proof, undermining fact,
its cruel accomplishment.
Something thrown, but where? Down, under,
into the suffering? As in *abduct, abuse.*

to Keith Sanborn

INSTRUCTION

To maximize the dim effects of dream
declaw the cat. Also,
name the mother in the dream, that one, spilling
on the first violinist in the quartet who sways in a crimson
gown. Or that one, sad on her cot
with only one eye, blinking at the wreath
hung on the wall where the fire was.
That is not a dream. Get rid of it.
To maximize the dim effects of dream
read Nabokov and listen to
rain. The woman with the long dark hair in the corner
was that the mother? The rich Christians in the west
speak in tongues. What do they say?
Are they speaking to God risen like a sun
over mountains? The mother was not there, so that also
is not the dream. Nabokov spoke in tongues, the hilarity of
his rue and rage teased from his mother's as from the milk
of human kindness. Drink the apparition.

EVENT HORIZON

1.

Lost reckoning *wing*   wing   side by side
measures the fleet's standard edition
                    atlas, bird, cup
one after another, so. The service policy
addressed all three, and credit
only the added attraction
unlisted except as an exclusive
so you needed cash in hand and a fast format

          If nothing resonates in this plot, try again.

But in order to find what we feel
is right, if it is right, we will need to make

                    whose
justification
may be the actual feeling
                              after
                                                  day or night.

                              Might there also be a scheme, a
contest, something to cover errors, make good
from the dump, find the thing
under the other things, one

that cannot be seen from here. Sing, brothers:
Dre e e   e am,
dream dream dream. Some
remain mute, wrapped
inside the hull
slow boat to *ch ch ch* agrees to trade invades *s s   s*
these are intimate sounds
and pictures lost behind clouds.

> *Power of Disney and the Pink Floyd oggles animated s s s*
> *graphic cats tinker toys inhabited archive*

Afloat, pushed to shore,
a pink shoe, a blond doll, personal stuff.
You might find me cast in that direction
breathing with difficulty
wishing never to find myself at sea again.

2.
The jokey ephemera of the age makes me believe
the birds are thirsty, pecking the dry bath.
What sweeps over the country
its glass eye, so that we see
through, but not into, ordinary habits of daily life?
The horizon, bewitched by fog,
caused them to spin

> *and took him down looking straight out at the dark ocean on a*
> *nearly moonless night get the wings level and find where*

as if in the shell of an egg.

The endeavor hid its tracks
in dissipated wonder
and they landed where the rubble left off—
far from the crowd
gathered at water's edge to watch the display.

Are you tired of all this happening?
The leaves appear to be tired; they have fallen to the ground.
Last night I counted
as they fell: one, two, three. The sky

    this bright economy

is tired of blue, now it is orange
with black spots. All else

    plus or minus the dials

is to be divided between theories of freedom
and theories of God

    tries to find a universal language what is his spirit
small integer absolute music forces of cacophony the danger of Futurism

depicted as lovers
slowly copulating on the sea's red and gold foam.

The best way to predict the future is to conceive it
    diehard merrily disconnects the chip

draw near
see the red tug the ruined castle double your anticipation.

3.

Enter the hero.

He grows up poorer than poor.

He ends up in a math class.

Even he doesn't believe it.

In six weeks

he would be more efficient.

He needed to create

a distraction.

He gets hooked up in Orlando.

It triggers expenditure, every big company,

you name it—

       close the door the fake participation of the manual laborer crime
hidden in Bond's site of production and human rights justice the Christian
                            and so on and so on
           order
  balanced order   Buddha for example coincidence of opposites wisdom in
favor of the good a collective of outcasts   beloved
                   liberation   tissue of spontaneity
                  hypersprecht

         O you who look for pastel transcendence
            who do not believe
      why imagine the white dot is a moon?
             Why slay the infidel?

There is no span

                              all arguments blur
                    and lower life mildews along the riverbank
                    and a figure goes on a rampage in the exhausted
                              vocabulary of displacement

                    the arc of the bridge has collapsed
                    things remain under their masks

                    there is neither the one nor the other with whom
                    to flirt. This is what occurs, less than a horizon

          tea leaves berserk in the global riverbed

Things drip.

4.

Another day's scansion

                              secretly at work in the massive affiliation

could focus
on an opening: icons appear for each thing: *atlas, bird, cup.*
Look up at the shape of a rotunda
humped high above the shore.
I was at the periphery all this time

all during this time I was at the periphery
notes fell through the percussive zeal

even as rose petals were strewn on the loading dock
and the bride kissed the groom
under their parasol

the issue of kids the lily project

mechanics of turbulence in the spheres
and the bleak continuum of a repeated phrase sung across the alley.

Clandestine erasures fortify our trivia, so this sheen, this look,
floats over rhetoric, beckoning small retrievals
onto which we might paste yet another history

might as well.

LOGISTICS

What are we to know? Inward, old seagull, cut,
abrasive magic and its clues. List
comes from the nearly invisible to announce
but she, in her museum of rhymes, finds death
among her things: inward, old seagull, and the numbers
cut out and the letters cut out.
There was a gathering. It was like a story, but not.
It was like another room in which Satie
was underlined in red, whose correction is
sate. So she might have been sated, in her notes,
her musical likeness, her
resistance. They were affiliated. That would be one
sentence to know.
But it would be trouble
when life depended on it.
If life depends on it. Life depends on it.
In noise, the mother said, *cut it out!*
wanting order and silence. But the mother was all
disorder and her nights were the noise of nights.

UNTITLED WITH MOON

What she sees are reinforcements from the dream
wherein the cat
comes out from under a flimsy wall
attached to its mother.
Better to lie down on the floor
and watch the canopy sway,
the logics of cloud tinker with light.

Tomorrow all stories will be abridged.
The old men will talk of creatures
bedazzled by dawn, the trick of dawn,
things unknown to anyone,
feuds and love confided by
uncle to girl when he feels the urge
to tell. Desire
will return, bounding or lancing down
from the scant universe, causing
burns and antennae,
blisters of air. The pilgrims will move on
into the funnel
cooled on the water by the moon's breath.
There is only one way down to the river, at least from here.

SEEN, OVERHEARD

To stay among shifts
      to fall out   beyond tools of trade
         beyond friendship's replicas
            her face turned
            his face

          among these
migrating references
              telephoto lens and
                offered spot

                ideal before murder
                ideal before the spoken

                        ideal before sport.

Yet the second galaxy is hazy to the naked eye
            bird blue
                to the eye up close   near the ground
                        near change.

Equation drowns from the corner
of an odd sensation
without a singular *and,* without addendum
so that
to live among these
to establish a plural
to race out from advice   a girl

                              spitting crumbs

        tit for tat   avarice of an already X-rated

                              schedule

                              personal story told at dinner among
                                              strangers.

Memory comes also
came along with
youthful impertinence
as of a boy sitting on a grave singing his *one two threes*
shot through with doubt.

Science came along only to aid method's imperative
those cruel and those careful
                              scribbles, tears
                              hours
        hunky-dory tryst   later a refrain   too easily stated
                              habitats of real time as opposed to

                                      routine

        the boy turns to tell his secret—

            Hamlet's affliction
                    sweet or imagined now

                                  as sweet.

FRAGMENT (AUGUST)

Look to turn more quickly toward   it was fetched   a remembrance
and the pervasive hinge

          a salutation   thunder, or betrayal, the lesser gods
              as uneasy as the greater, their saga inconclusive, their minds
              unmade up.

The greens hung

              lofty, low—

It was not a city to be known by heart.
It was not a small town.
The sea was elsewhere, crashing up against dunes.
It was merely an afternoon
                    contaminated on either side—

HARMONY

Truculent thing
why missing from these premises?
Stuck in abstraction, in the coiled hand?
Why feeble as you jog along the streets?
Why almost touching?
Are you Socrates, to be written
into the season of robins and suicide?
Is your pose characteristic?
Did you inherit the magenta ring
or the trees' wild seizure,
the rival architect's house
hardly built but shining?
Toddler call, at variance with icons,
are you indifferent to sorrow?
Relic of mismanaged risk
newly made, are you,
have you already been forgiven?

COUNTRY LIFE

And lived differently, in a crude cul-de-sac,
with the mangy fox and his id
a clown. Another old horse, this one
made from plastic and wire, trudged out
to find a mare, not aware that war was immanent
and he would be asked about his expenditures
in the star-cast anthem of restitution. The kids were
out of school and on their motors, tearing through the brush,
hell-bent on speed, ignoring the gold birds and their song.
They would never ask who the girl is in the poem, the one in which
Stevens intones a greater mystery, they would not want to know
about mystery. They would want to ride until they won.
And the old clown would want to swoon.

Desire comes and goes and comes,
as if wings on a stem in late summer. The wind came
pretending to be spirit, its largesse vaulting day
and leaving twigs scattered on the grass. That was a good sign,
in a time without signs. It was hard to say, given that no one
read signs any more, except Children At Play and
Stop The Plant. The train was famously remote, and beautiful in its
roar along the river's edge, hooting and dragging its hoot through air.
And still the issues arose urgently, unlike the night, ever calm.

OPPEN'S WAY

A small table is not a vacancy.
I promise to avoid quotation.

Look what you have started.
Is there another word for Patrick?

But she is singing again!
How much was the farm in Vermont?

To the right is a landscape in Iceland.
My grandfather's ketch was called *Hawkbells*.

The forsythia screams on the hill.
I am trying to drink more water.

I see the bell but only by looking up.
Now everything is wet.

If I change my ways will the way change?
He sailed with his wife, Mary.

Memory is a form of forgetting.
I am talking a lot in my sleep.

Clarity in the sense of silence.
Now I have done it again.

to Patrick Farrell

SIGN

Beware of accidents, they will bring grief to paintings.
Beware of the shrub, it will grow into bronze.
Beware of the young, they will leave your food.
Beware of those who take notes, they will cancel your silence.
Beware of red lace, it will turn into film.

Beware of the father, he will teach you to build.
Beware of the brother, he will answer in jargon.
Beware of the mother, she will ruin the meadow.
Beware of the sister, she will dig up your shoes.
Beware of the lover, he will abstract your love.

AFTER MAHLER

A thousand minutes came out of the tottering state.
The bed of thyme moved within its bearings like a dream.
He answered, *tomorrow.*
Someone else was screaming on the radio; people laughed.
The cat has been dead for some time now.
The wedding party's bright joy looked strange from the streaking jet.

Meanwhile persons are moving around outside. They have decided to
                                        foreclose on
options pertaining to the new world. Instead, to allow themselves to
                                    live in a world
neither new nor old, but which abides as in a balloon floating
untethered above trophies and noise so that
                                        wren-shrunk

Pentecostal shade
                harp rubbed   under Mahler's tent   (his abundant farewell
                    to Alma's rage)
        after all   the part that was said and the part that was done
                the conductor in his care   so one was forced to go
                    back
                to how it might have begun   after all
                    the century that leaks its tunes into the summer air
                    refuses to call
                        to call is to ask   break a silence   but the
                                        music

after all it is music   song-spiraled
    and the landscape detained   across a field   into a night
                                in which we
learn only the pornography of sight
    its ocular target

                    see see see

    from above the tents and the persons milling about
    in their robes

                 they are the disciples! silence them!

        And if they are merely birds   flocks rising in circles
like smoke without song   *see see*
    we cannot hear the tremulous strings   nor the soprano   glittering
        in the heat of the tent
        the conductor mouthing her words   not that.

Sun, making its way east and east and west of the river
where the ivy is not poison and the trees not weeds. And
this or that spins into
the final cycle, its systemic will. Do not butter the toast, do not come
like a ghost without shame, a promise adumbrated
against the cry of any nocturnal creature.
All against one, and the philosophical questions
on a far continent like so many markets.

Not that either.

Conditions above the smashed agora with the cowboy riding sunset on his
mechanical cart, his small mouth and child's
incontinent whine. Casinos in full play, paying for
assault, moving to the rush of coin. And still we did not speak, did
not know to whom to speak, muttered at lunch, gave each other
proofs of care, one to
one, but did not come to the table to hear our fathers, they were dead, our
mothers, they were busy, our neighbors, they were
elsewhere, our lovers, they
were not listening. Listen. This is a lullaby. Listen.

to Leon Botstein

OPERA

Logic, for example, skewed from mooring.
Boats adrift but loaded.
Anchors away! *This way*, says the captain,
this way, says the mate.
That said, the small grows
into film and an audience forms to clap.
For the good guy.
For the wounded under a halo of sand.
Bands play. Flags. Aromas.
The blackened fields ready for grafting,
seeds incapacitated
in the nuance of tragedy
stripped to its bone—
disinclined to repeat
unworthy of sequence.
A monotone of commitment.
Thus illogic disguised as logic.
Thus Faust through the ages.
And the heart's munitions
cooked down to devotion, seared in a pot.
Pot of melted weaponry.
The margin called to from afar.
Speech acts.
Massive audience turning away in tears.
The nonmoon followed by the nonsun.

Two

IMPOSSIBLE BLUE

STONES (THE COAST OF TURKEY; ROBERT SMITHSON)

1.

Forget that version, gist's
truncated eruption, stone
placating heat, avenue luminous but forbidden
up the steep assault. She of glittering rings, of the swollen
intricacy of faith, sinks into dust, frees an icon from its
distillation—unction of tears, waxy scent
of a remnant nave. Out there, things ride their riddles
like toys in space, an agenda gap on the morphic tide.
Here, the soul pivots on scripted discs
curving away from the story
we thought we would always tell.
Bird, halo, gust,
Poseidon grass and impeccable weave
(silk on silk) young sailor with one leg raised,
the bride stalked, red beads
hurting her throat.

Now a veil
is thrown clear across the disturbance
across the domestic stage
to the circle's wet edge.
I can see through this, and this, I can see
the dispersal as if it were tomorrow, hinge of arrival opening—
how it goes, adage after adage, through the sanctuary,

the nave's arcade,
dipped pigment and last trace
trespassing over a bridge onto a continent, the increments
bewildered by detail—
searching the site,
mouth, thumb, foot,
stone angled across the processional
where they climb to stare, the him and the her,
black goats bleating from the cloister
passing something on.
Single plaintive note, little redundancy.

2.

The arcade leads
from sacred to secular, carrying the relic
overhead, architect
hammering away at bedrock, swallows
igniting air's scripture,
sediment extended outward and down—
nudity of the example, its accumulated rite.

In this space, glyphs
transcribe scale's precision.
This or that step
falters at the bazaar,
postcards fall through the mosque's vaulted diaspora,
releasing their images from history's
crude hideout,

mistakes and dead-ends
in peripheral vision—men hugging each other
while another, bloody scrap on the road, is perpetually beaten.
There was the illusion of purpose, the illusion of content,
as if we were responses annulled by our norms.
Hired old dame weaving,
raw wool pulled through
a tourist economy,
its itinerant, spectral, real.

A false god has a greater reality than the true,
and *so extensions of the Cartesian mind are carried to the most*
attenuated points of no return
babbles the anthropologist
as a young man wraps a car in cloth
to mourn the contemporary, his desire
kept under the revolution's chronic restatement, tour guide
speaking in third person, bus of strangers
importuned with tea.

                              The impure surface,
iridescent purple, green and silver surfaces,
these surfaces disclose a cold scintillation,
sight is abolished by a hermetic kingdom of surfaces.
The surfaces of the reliefs are definitely surfaces,
the surfaces in Scorpio Rising,
or California surfaces, the
brilliant chromatic surface—Thanatos in aqua,
surfaces that look mineral hard. A variety of surfaces

from Saturnian orchid-plus to wrinkle-textured blues and greens,
the inside surfaces of the steel sites,
every surface in full view.

3.
Comatose vision
etched in a mirror

sleep extends its tale
deprived of solace

the dream's epithet
profits us not

sweltering veil
veranda backlit

and her hair
measured for afterlife

the Sultan's concubine
kept in a cage

heat's fiasco
forensic pursuit

huge jewels
perfectly arranged

the dialogue stymied
at the mark of lost faith

4.

I saw a young boy in a row boat but he did not see me.

Chaste catastrophe of a broken mast
                                    men holed up in the mountains
                        to travel as lightly as snow
                            to fall
                                    upon fact

Already a tool's coercion
reels with annunciations
of some one or thing. A yellowy
dross fades into apertures
whose program is scuttled—
diadems for children
made to fall apart.
O spiral of light!
The petals fall, water
dull scum. Once
among these you thought
shadow nerves would come alive
but the body is a fetish: all its moments sealed in a box.
Perhaps the sculptor's last nobility
gives something back, like the moon to a landscape.
The old knight, there in dark garb, peers at the abstinent blank.
We can make things look natural, but that doesn't mean they are.

We had told the story of
restoration, pasted the new leaf on the tree.
A belated significance forecasts
its currency, as if among figments
we might enter the glare where history collapsed,
catalyst dispersed as the unremembered,
one ruin much like another, one choice
for a better tomorrow: mass appeal, filling station, chorale.
And the hostage figure—transference and mechanism
caught by intention's blind noise, site newly animate—claims its form.

MEMENTO MORI (BERLIN)

Kept or held in *help me* position
and she
to whom the cry is cast
is dead.
Wheels on gravel.
Dog.
The season with a hole in its side.
Intercepted, hand out
as if one could know, or come to know,
in the city, walking among lit staves
among young girls with silver flutes
playing snippets of Mozart, gilt embellishments of the castle,
dust along water's edge, pool
of fat children, vicissitudes of gray
in the crypt, the new museum's
horde of old art,
the rip, breach, wound and
the hope
to make it up or rebuild or draw
in the day the things that belonged to the night:
cartoons, scaffolds,
tones massed in the bell tower, ruin
at the intersection,
walls picked like bad skin,
things literal or not, so
you think *sign,*
mechanical thing,

and the angel on the plinth
its geography faltering like a compass
circumventing distance
in the place of the double moon and the silent skiff
impasse clustered over the kiln,
bony intervention, Darwin's worms impeded,
and still the light
still the harpy comes blistering out of the crowd
to interrogate the boy,
to ask for papers, name, occupation
let me not forget.

So this is the zone of lost calls.
Or the allegiance to the gymnast
under the hood of the BMW, or
Wagner's immensity.
There is a squirrel in the birdbath, the evening
broken in branches of maple.
Of things barbaric, ideal.

IMPOSSIBLE BLUE

The blue   there are no slippers   phoned from the street
the countess   a walk across the bridge   finding a dress and shoes
the black shoes   transparent   raining on snow
the birds   to be ready for the dance   the second wife
came back   sailing   the blue
the bridge in gold light
the birds in snow
you telephoned
I said I would I
did not   the blue   after crossing

And that the obscure would approach
in crystal sheaves
accumulating but
undressed, denuded
as of spines or wires or where
there cannot be a mirror
only the blankly encumbered mass
as when the sitter closes her eyes
the veins under skin
or the person falls
the kitchen tile on her cheek.

That the obscure
approaches with mere crutches, polished,
and the title of a book

or the blank inside of the book
or the recollected word.

There is no telling, except by the analogy of the snow
and the embarrassed receptor
embodied, so one imagines a shell in a tree
as bells chime discursive thirds.
The stones will return, their
old grammar
leaked upward through snow.
And there, a bench, a path.
Birds, or shoes, on the hill.

I cannot say
how the vanishing
turns to a sign for blue after it has left
only the light by which it became blue
as a body makes a sign
lifting the hand
turning the head.
And the stamp in the snow
is, we say, a footprint
down into the blue
print in the snow
or of the snow
noticed, the requisite
agreement, and the normal
progress from snow to blue to cold
logic, without argument, open to shut
like curtains but not

how the dream has
no proof of its objects, not
how the world folds into speechlessness
how the silk curtains are enflamed
feeling in the folds of the silk curtains
untranslatable effects
as if we could touch the light
pick it up and put it in the mouth
exhale audible shade,
the deepest blue, say you
saying *I* say you.

to Norma Cole

ABOUT THE DARKNESS OF
THE SELF, AWKWARD (GIOTTO)

Fear arguably
nobody's name, nothing abstract

taking place in the extended

      correlates to sabotage   the villain

  sham
      the elicited shame

a politically other   condition   sabotage   or heterogeneous zone
        things begin by falling, have fallen

into soul's pivot
so proximate to skin
you might say, credo held
back from the image of the dark
having fallen and the bats' high swirl after dark
additive but not ordinary, like care, how we care,
he going into the undark room with the books
you into yours, I to mine, to our rooms

        false water burbles incessantly
        around fake fish

        to save the light

against art, against nature also, if nature is not false
and if art is true
to something
to some thing or some one, some one thing
estimated to be

     true water, a river for example, under a bridge

        so much water under the bridge is how the past
        is said to become itself

the eventful slosh
about which we can do nothing

how to make something from the nothing under the bridge

how to cross
to that side of the bridge
           to not let the saying
              sabotage, not be afraid to cross
                 the delinquent clarity of dark

                passing
            under the
bridge

He built a house within a house
into which certain tenants enter
so we might speak about the true cost
of making something

                              awkwardly, self
                                        turns from natural dark
                              to an architecture

              reads in a room
                    as the sun sets, the setting

on the other side of the river
that side or *your* side

the birds, you said
have not all left for the winter

you said nothing about the fish

                              dark shelter as the soul pivots
          miraculously

          to Assisi
          earth into earth falling

          you also said we do not yet know what conditions

          cause *Giotto*, the form of life *Giotto*

          to be present

                    in bewildered adjacency, erupting,
                    as a bird from water

                                                      a few egrets and gulls

and were shown photographs taken by the now dead artist of herself
collected in a book
and were shown the guest house.

                    to Michael Brenson

DETAIL 858-6
(GERHARD RICHTER)

1.

    Aspiring glance   bound force   array
        turns of glass   how
              charged by reflection
to travel quick   toward   undone
        singular stroke

                syntax unanchored
to recognize   *blur*
        notes on a scaffold   metonymy's grace
to alter narrative adjacent to cause

            ripple
        close-up fracture   ream   patch   flare
            mineral strata
                under skin

    shade
        forged by a figure of day
     ragged impediment to horizon's door

    the lewd sun's encrypted ease   risen over sand
        boned sky adrift
    vertigo meaning   invention's wound and peel
the transitive eye   *insight to insight*   now
        hinged open
           foray begun.

2.

How?　　　to ask how
persuasion　　begets
material inventory　　you sample you measure　your

　　　　　　　phase　　within passion　　　　　locale
　　　　without gate　　rift　　exit　　breach

　　　　　　　　　　　lesion map　　faces
　　　　　a matrix of leavings
　　　　　　　　　cycle of flaws attached to　*the possible*
　　　　　　　　　　　　attached to transit
　　　　　　　the body present　the chance remark
　　　　　　　　　　intimate answer
　　　　　　　　　　　　quotidian care.

3.

　　　　　　　　　Meanwhiles
fluttering　　wingnote　*fl fl fl*
　　　　grasp the instant's sleeve
add　　looking at through
　　　　　　　trace imperatives　at arm's length
　　　　　　　　　　　　or form
　　　　a beleaguered architecture
wall　field　edge

　　　　　　　　　　　micro-scale
　　　　　　rivets　　windy doubt
　　　　　　　　　fragment one
　　　enters

presently

a ground of objects

latent in underbrush   among strangers   in the roaming view

hope's knot tied in radiant fabric

ordinarily an interior well

response to response

secular gift
labor for ours.

GRID MTV

Singly, out of blank, singly
as when *never* opens an eye
under the stressed
staring bud
weaves out chords
that some were insisting is music.
Not the simple reactionary sway of horizon—
freighted substitutions, Chinese shorts, panic roofs—
what were these but a pastel charity, sneaker prints
on a book jacket? Holes in
snow, what were they? Thimbles.
As if "life" could touch its metaphors, concentration
bring itself to an afterimage,
break apart, unravel,
and we still on the inside of now
where the house itself is occupying the house
with only a flickering sense
of what memory might look like from here:
"before the fact" "Berlin" "the same chalk."
Repetition is the wager of abstraction, Stephen said,
painting over and under, transgression without force.

Here is the fluid violence of wealth, white fence
lacing humped largesse, toes
bright in
snakeskin mules,
the new world's acts

coming in close, diamond pupils,
among crass
disadvantages, schematic
list, bower of chores, to dress
the imbecile in silk
the sick in the nude restlessness
of a summer night, the stars having fallen onto the meadow
in bug scraps, graves tilting, oaks opulent and straight,
the punishing vocabulary of ease pulled from the dump.
The sun might be a slingshot heaven, raking the world,
besotted with damp.

Please do not hurt the ghost's sealed amphitheater, not sky,
not bright strips above the broken instance of love,
not this unanswered provocation from afar
pulling twilight, as the girl her mother's hair.
Fractions of money launch
a pure ambition to receive, and I
am confounded in this exercise of rooms, whose brother
steps into water to skip stones. The inundated horizon,
its gift? Counting up from year to year
at the edge of the graveyard where the raccoon crossed, where the crows
speak their condition, where wandering beasts are a currency of error.

Who lost? Under night gun, trees
emanating faint fingers,
sun impossible, sun bewildered, sun
clasped at the root of the mountain's blue,
sun under impossible fingers, rising

to the vagrant collisions of being,
mind, you would say, wondering if the subject were that,
or other impossible gifts
their commerce wholly measured.
Ladies and gentlemen, rock 'n roll.

to Stephen Westfall

TRIANGLES AND SQUARES
(GUSTON, MALËVICH)

1.

Age willow   approach the normal   she is leaving

    she has turned her back

        not yet abysmal   thwarted   going forth going forth away

           and the scene   hard not to miss coming down the aisle
           triangular   two women and a man
                         hood
               pyramid

                    we have seen this shape in space

    the stars invent it

    there were furies too in her stripped descent
                before the blockade

    she came down frontally

       and the three
             the subtle dementia   forget its origin
               green will set it aflame
       quash the dissonant hulk

the triangle grips its tilt

                             in the neighborhood of siblings
                                      their secrets

                 so that
      "doubt itself becomes form."

          Shoe heel shoe   spiral confession follows a dotted line.

Talk about green
salvaging the crude
vicissitude of steady shapes
discover the horizon's
rubble of butts.

      There will be surprise now in going away after they reach the floor
      prize of the incipient link

      although things continue to swell beyond their geometry
      and we continue
      to be afraid

      this would be bald in the face of the critic
      the embedded brush spitting

          some spurious indictments occur
          followed by redemptive privilege.

Would they be counted?
Have the steps been counted?

2.

Cohort under sky
teeter the mongrel cat, teeter reliance
upriver the spoon catches a glint   eyebrow   moon bugged
the woman asking about happiness as if it were how

                                    dealing out the days
                                            one two three
                    the double play
                            jeopardy of underwritten love

                                        asleep under the line
                                        in a cartoon bed.

All loosely knit   nearby a keg ready to go
thump thump the display
thrum the old beat
sleeping against the grain of the mildewed plank
where the adventure went amiss, where the story got lost
as she stood on the burning deck like an angel on film.
Comes to an end. Disestablished path *maybe baby*
token analytic muse in the glove compartment.

3.

The roses are desolate in their insufficient arrangement.
The subject grows old. The subject may or may not be roses.
A matter of toes, of the small bones in the fingers,
torque of hip, the face down,
abrasive voice collapsing into the lover's ear.
The women frail, not listening to praise, there is not enough
to undo the arrangement in the jar.
The certitude of the arrangement in the pastel jar.

The meadow will not come forth from the meadow,
adjacency falters at the supplicant's will.
It, the meadow, embodies only space
crouching and malingering there,
the diatribe of the unmolested in its manifest lust.
Yes come, yes go, yes die, yes the pretty fern
yes the geometric sun, yes the line of abstraction, o yes
monster ambition flourishing, violent inhuman field
annealed to the human. Road. Blue house. Sign.

The threesome is neat   love moves easily among its angles
the fourth part is absent   we reject its shape
the fourth part rolls down the coast
Malëvich refutes it   follow along the signs of its elision
the square was only

a boy with his knapsack
a woman crossing his path.

to Augusta Talbot

PREY (BOTTICELLI)

To walk slowly behind
and so to be late

too late to take cover
too late for alms

so slowly
drops drilled into snow

not mistaken for tears
not made into fuel

slowly behind the engine
guided ahead

to wonder if the dream
is guided to its end

to speak aloud to the dream
at the curb of dawn

its bag of spoils
to talk slowly

standing behind
the man looking down

do not kill the man
as he bows in prayer

the ambush
within the walls

the eyes of the child
photographed again

still too late
without counsel or means

shabbily attired
shoeless in a park

on the streets with no name
in the country of *The*

to look at his neck
at the coil of his hair

the arc of his brow
his deliberate lips

to wonder how his voice said
this is this, this is not

something must survive
be found under snow

the cloth
the glass

the bag
the cup

may as well
wake to the voice

not interfere
not yet be part

the aftermath
of what was done, what not

a percentage or guess
far from the source

about the shoe in the landscape
walked to its end

stems
static in snow, the enemy *the*

awaiting internment
things of the world

always too late
to turn

away from the flight
path and roof

infinite sand, infinite ice
too late

to resist the zone
the brow of a hill

the open eyes
the dump of the dead.

to Mark Costello

BOOKMARK, HORIZON
(EMILY DICKINSON,
JOSEPH CORNELL)

Where whatever the *blue* was
found its hesitancy as pierced inscription
                    drew dispersal

back through the sieve toward the eye's
singular vantage

                    face of a girl
                              and the first room on the top floor
                              "1425"

                    the glossed immersion
                    as if a jar could open space

                              aught in the old vitrine
              thwart cobalt
              thwart the incipience of cloud, and the leftover, omitted arc
                              a rig for flight

which might have been a habit of scale
or the fast stopped by your gaze

what stalled? the glassy circumference?
the dainty primer of decay? inquisitive ink drained from sound?

the room enlarged beyond fog, beyond the bending annotated way
unbound by its wall, where *l'etoile*
is embossed on the stationery
and the sign is dry—

turn, brief volition, at the far shore.

Three

HUM

TO & SO

Unalterable complex   unfurled shed.
        Came this way   unslithered
        purchase factored in
          as
          noise (following personal
  revelations of the suit)
        swiftly, swiftly   "then"
          glazed over visual
      to
          amplitude of signs
  crank imperatives   tide of ephemera
        held or foretold

to
the graduated sweetness of an impasse
swindle, cant, ribs cut out

       to

          episodes O! O! O!

      the reporter is lonely in Istanbul?
       carpets, tea, blue glass, bridge

   to

perfect these

        household gods

    eyes against envy, beads against expectation

       more stones, letters
       and so
the symmetry of good windows set

to

    recall, in distant times,
    how facts

      looked blank, under thrall
       of prerequisite doubt.

     Nothing defraged there, only terse contractions
     enjoyed up close

     riddle, whim
     apparition
       clear-eyed, yes, but something
       seduces even the greatest soldier

to minor treason—

       infatuated
       tables slanted up, legs raised

a motion of tears
quotidian exhaled

a farewell of sorts
under logic, under guess, where the bug
without much left
its all
too small

diligent marker

shipwrecked encyclopedia

coyote racing across a graveyard toward a flock of wild turkeys.

2.
OK, so

here is rain's
insistent oblique

elderly contest
she who would have seemed

before this task
had resembled, but now

abstract, global
an abbreviated cost

there will be no generals
in our army of thieves

and the big library
will discover little poems

there is always violence
and clean elaboration of such.

What? What?
You want to ask *what?*

3.

Unjust equation   night *is* night

        closes on a simple thing
        recurrent in the kneeling air

        collapse of particulars   say leaf say drip
        what is required is attached at the outer rim

        we in our love
                        also indicted
        because the frame extends only so far
        then around a corner then descent
        gradual glide into viscous air.

Up again? Is this another never,
another cell, another impossible procedure, another
X, another unsayable,

thread lifted from a wall
steel arc leaning in the public arena
surface wax
doctrinal silence

huge installation of the instant
hardly any water

eyes of the rat
where there was rain.

Unmanageable   clock   partition   murmur
sincere, sincere   what is it you want?
beyond delusion's skin, the characteristic eye
staring out again
fractured road   glossy   ravenous with suction

images among graves

so

apart from what you were saying
the tie looms
contaminated by what is not
sullied by sport

slender hands of the brute
dusting his lapels

                      so

unmoved   enchantment   as myth
unpinned   fallen   as wound
sojourn of the various   ablaze a cloister exhumed
        a cradle dumped
    darkened then darkened   entrance glued to endurance
                  so

   you had to mention the will

                so

   were led away

   doorstep forbidden
   disestablished strip of the radiant plenum

                          bare-shouldered, strapless, sky.

VICTORY

Reverence for that dust.
The scale is overwhelming. I
cannot envision this ever getting done.
They took a lot away from us.
World rattles its harness.
Among, within us, too many injuries
as if in caves in mountains in snow. The train
whistled, a thing of air,
and the chorale also ceased.
Night took over even as the moon
came up blushing and round to lead us on.
The philosopher with the poker was in a rage.
Sebald perished in a crash. I looked up
to find the stars rambling across the sky and
that morning the starlings,
the starlings, I have nothing to say about starlings.

The body does not appear; enthusiastically, the guitar strums.
Shoes wander; vertiginous ascent, pathology of disorder
in which nothing is under the overlay
of a high-velocity near. The kids are on their snowmobiles.
I could kill them. I could speak of killing the kids
and not mean it. I could kill the snowmobiles
and ask the kids to look at the copulating
dolls hung from threads
and then at solace.

If form is recurrence, who sighs at the
spoken? *Ah ah ah,* the anecdotal takes
sunset and moonrise into a regime.
To speak outside the retro-fit of
a target's eye, blinking, hands waving as the ship pulls out,
empathy like a shadow on an object's pyre,
the object's stench
as the crowd presses
to climb the platform, snap the shutter,
watch it burn.
                    Duration slit open?
Whiplash speed rising over the skull
as an idea, any idea, say a mask,
and the shreds now
catapulting our pleasure
into this
fissure or slit through which the eye
perpetuates its claim
and all it sees is
limitless enunciation, limitless screen,
undone by the actual yet called up by
readiness: cloth, snow, page,
trees at dusk ready to disappear.
The monochrome tugs at its frame.
The news will not assuage, greets
the about-turn reckoned
as victory's norm
or sample contingent: in wartime,
reporters eat in or at the house of the vanquished.

FIELD

And then the threshold's disobedient ink
traces the surprise of reproduction

to an adamant closure:
a child hides in dust.

As appetite subsides
intention is obscure. The blinds buzz.

Bald branches twitch.
Nature casts doubt onto the thing,

its rueful target begets a toy.
Kill! cries the child, practicing,

as the globe
spins into vagrant cosmology.

TWIG

Coming toward herself
mumbling they would say
the occupied nude

and the wretched antecedent
hair on white linen
the calibrated source

waving as she had waved
a flag or a scarf
and had fainted into dew

the stains of dew.
Once water had carried

the photon crypt
its surplus song

a riot of figuration
stranded

because she had come to rest
or was blinded or woke up.

FRAGMENT (SEPTEMBER)

Filtered through the cast of *happiness* so that
evening has the weight of unconditional assent
beyond the debris

HUM

The days are beautiful.
The days are beautiful.

I know what days are.
The other is weather.

I know what weather is.
The days are beautiful.

Things are incidental.
Someone is weeping.

I weep for the incidental.
The days are beautiful.

Where is tomorrow?
Everyone will weep.

Tomorrow was yesterday.
The days are beautiful.

Tomorrow was yesterday.
Today is weather.

The sound of the weather
is everyone weeping.

Everyone is incidental.
Everyone weeps.

The tears of today
will put out tomorrow.

The rain is ashes.
The days are beautiful.

The rain falls down.
The sound is falling.

The sky is a cloud.
The days are beautiful.

The sky is dust.
The weather is yesterday.

The weather is yesterday.
The sound is weeping.

What is this dust?
The weather is nothing.

The days are beautiful.
The towers are yesterday.

The towers are incidental.
What are these ashes?

Here is the hat
that does not travel.

Here is the robe
that smells of the night.

Here are the words
retired to their books.

Here are the stones
loosed from their settings.

Here is the bridge
over the water.

Here is the place
where the sun came up.

Here is a season
dry in the fireplace.

Here are the ashes.
The days are beautiful.

ELEGY IN AUGUST

Guess again at the brown bird's cue. It is dry.
It is dry again, and so also still dry. So dry
it could be a French repetition, not weather at all.
These filmic follies. These skirmishes/décor
of the flat-chested actress with thin lips.
Enhancement of the singular does not count
or else this is an event among thieves
and the women who belong to the thieves.
So dry, so many, so common. The twilight brown bird.
The accretion of musical numbers. Counting, so.

But garden! Only hymns and slight poems to praise you
to your grave? But garden! We were there, we listened.
Michael had been invited to a convocation. He is
adored in other countries.
Michael! Only hymns and slight poems.
Only counted stones.
But garden!
And yet, in the heady nomenclature of the newly dead
there are forgotten words. *Hollyhock, cornflower, foxglove.*
I dare you. I dare you to unplant the daisies
under glass. Only white flowers grow. But Michael!

Mais jardin, Angel. Is a season
coming next or easily stranded
with the worried bird?
The brown bird, twilight, the white flame.

Is reason coming? Is this your curtain?
To be so lovingly displayed as Michael's worth
(lilies, Queen Anne's lace)
with the night-eyed ghost.
Planted these. Is it your garden?
Stone arch, bed, broken root.
Is it your garden? Your twilight?
The roses were stolen from China, with tea.

in memory of Margaret Schaffer

TOPOS

The dream modifies   not you but your hand
across the anomaly

               between question and answer

neither to say nor to write   betrayals.

     But the end of day is

                also unsayable, and so
     I think
         this is not funny, or I do not find it funny, and
          you may wonder what *this* or *it* might be.

              To come upon the bird at its bath.
     To say

       I love you

            to find or think *I love you*
        where you and I are not here
in the way the bird is not here and cannot know this love.

     So we inscribe that which is

               she was weeping
        at what made
          father and mother? Those?

          I said these words

                                          but which body?

                 The world's voices?

        Plural wandering   a thief has stolen files
                                              along with the headset

                      another synecdoche   one thing stands for another or for all

        the deer's antlers
        painted as branches   the black painting the violent colors   "sunset"
                          mythic proportions so that we can say Icarus
                   or tell of the lover   or tell of the tower or tell of the father

                    fires sending smoke to our sun
                                              plural wandering
                          as if the stones might know

                          how the brow of the hill
                          the bedrock
                          cropping out from vintage grass like a head

                          a fossil of
                          kind.

        To be on the ship   to have been on the island
                                              to encounter the island
                          to suggest the island
                   a conceptual accident   a version   no more than a version

                                        of sunset.

And so we come across the credentials of the moon.

An insubstantial but visible *more*
its augmented sum
another guide or force

                the difference between a guide and a force might be
            between science and myth
            or a teacher and wind.

I am thinking this after Garrett came on his motorcycle
and headed back down to the city toward the end of day

I had said if we omit the subject
and speak only the language of form

if the girl painting knows paint
and the boy writing knows words

but she has nothing to paint and he has nothing to say
how can meaning be made?

Form is responsive to subject
or subject to form

when they merge, content is made, content
is the merger of subject with form.

If subject remains only subject
if form is only form

there is no content, and no meaning
can come to those who look

or those who listen or to those who read.
These are necessary attachments.

to Garrett Kalleberg

SELF-PORTRAIT AS I AM

Not the law
abiding here, embodied, decorative
end-papers resembling Jackson Pollock's *Painting No. 2* but
unfinished, pausing on the trek up the mountain for honey
an error on the dial and so
the person who no longer kisses on the mouth
the reason for that
visitor, as we are, moving through
but not wind

                astonished at

                   wild fire   this is an image of direction

                       so the songs go and so
fires
           some ashes on paper, the sun

           yellowish on its way down   it has no sound   the heat
                                abating   is local

              without spectacle
                 but the roads

but the roads are cool

                    traversing the expectant

        one has witnessed it

                        it and other its   all those
                                    licensed to
proceed
        from what speaks to what is   the homily endorsed   and heat

                in the home stretch unmitigated by lost immunity

and the also lost injunction to protest
on the day reserved for protests, yesterday,
in the thrall of June
when we waited for the call,
words easily assayed in the forgiven, by way
of local trade: *I love you, I love you too*
as if this were a fact with the consequences of fact
where one might quote Arendt, her dissertation on Augustine,
By desiring and depending on things 'outside myself,' that is, on the very
                                    things I am
not, I lose the unity that holds me together by virtue of which I can say 'I am.'
Or one of the texts garnered from the ancients,
something from Thomas, the disciple whose gospel was lost,
who wanted to put his finger in the Wound, who
pulled the beam from water.

Jesus said: If you bring forth that which is within yourselves,
That which you have will save you.
If you do not have that within yourselves,
That which you do not have within you will kill you.
When I was young I began to draw.
This was after the incomprehensible occurred.
A drawing of a creature with enflamed wings. I believed it could fly.

GOD

Pulled   against a gaudy *predicament*   *gaudy* a lance or trap
    up from the sequel   not to point exactly but give
    direction from the underworld
        gaudy an appraisal from above looking down at oceans lit or at
    her great ring on its envy finger

"predicament" as was being said before the talk
after the ease coming up against this
maw of shine, abundant also in a direction
where you could say form is what repeats itself
or what inhabits the sign of its meaning
predictable, yes, the graveyard only a stone's throw from my throat
glad to be smiled upon even by those
       who know nothing of our latest crimes
         stealth, lies, cruelty, women stoned, girls stolen, one abuse after—

A doll, let's say again a doll, dressed in her conceit dress,
flounced, elaborately tied, buttons, bows,
tiny underthings, smalls and smaller smalls, white socks,
black shoes with laces. It
does not age, it fades, molds, rips in the ways that beset things.
Is this a lyric? Can you tell me if this is a lyric?
It is about a doll, which is a thing and also an image, one
kind of thing image. Anyway, there is a doll.
A "female," or else a cross-dresser, doubtful, but
an interesting idea for an image.
You would have to lift up her petticoats.

Is this the same doll? Is it archival?
Is it part of a collection, people have collections of dolls,
they are serial doll lovers.
I have had many dolls, and many lovers.
Does this make me a lyric poet?
Am I singing now, the way the doll might have sung
something from "Guys and Dolls," a musical,
in which there were lyrics I once knew by heart.
If I know things by heart, does this make me a lyric poet?

If I substitute the word "God" for doll, does that make me a religious poet?
"They are serial God lovers."
"I have had many gods, and many lovers."
"Something from Guys and Gods, a musical."
"Am I singing now, the way God might have sung?"
In this substitution, a gull flies out,
and it cries real tears. Does this make me a nature poet,
a metaphysical poet? A god is an intellectual thing.

M. AND F. AT THE K.G.B.

Trickily absorbed into ekphrastic juvenalia
shot from the hip. Think I'll listen to Emmy Lou
before the fervor of the andante.

Shostakovich, plural and harmonic
but repeated over there, in the mud
with young boys and their tools, their faces

sweating with boundary.
Old goat's lust for the worldly arena.
A woman of emendation, a man of domestic glass

came to speak to us before our trip,
upbraid our vague dilemmas
and such quotidian enunciations as the Dow

beyond what we might have witnessed
in the early homespun riot
before the colossal carried us off into infrastructure

inverting the usual designation of
girl-boy trials—she
tracks the insignia of thought, thinks the bleachers

will hold, he would open each flower, blossom
in the appellant of a kindly disciple: Moses, one shoe off,
rises to the tinsel bush. She is

recursive, belonging to an addition, like a
good logic, marries Mayakovsky to the sublime
as she submits her laws to our court.

His entreaty to come through the kitchen door
rivals concordance, and so
they agree: *trot trot trot* to a different beat.

PRECISION TUNING

Curtailed argument for small   alert
less than alert   contaminated
                                  singular
        came as thought
thought contrived instances of good
the good night captured
illegally captured   drawn smoke
without looking up smoke rises through slots
drastic in the slotted spoon or held
Annunciation's drastic fidelity
still following as faithful thought
hurt its lungs, slept.

Such incipience must conjure new ordeals
ordeals specific to this
this being troubled by sanction
so that the sanctions come from above
as if rain, from above but superimposed.

The superior army imposed
the prohibited calm
those who erase the calm rims of Enlightenment
those who spend secular gold, light

those who omit light

                    who wear the feeble shawl of sobriety
his mother in shawls
father in custody
the family custodian arranged chronologically
without deviation   children   first second third
trays of numbered slaughter.

XYZ PLUS MINUS

X

(   ) settles in
mirage person go! go!
be punctuated be
adroit
       (   ) settles
dead one dead three

thou sand thou one   in the desert
hi!

           (   ) settles

why these should be removed
and these later
this plus this

you have too many in your program
you have too many (   ) in your (   ).

and the exception to this rule is? And this object?
We recommend you
furnish (   ) with another
and that you buy only what is
transparent to the

the eye.
Is the eye a good judge?

Y

Knot.
Aha, a little
jokey pun.
Jokes are a good thing
under conditions of the non-joke.
To untie the knot.
Now?

The heart is
awakened by a small
mis-
take or de-
lay or am-
big-
u-
ity. Do you want to save
the ex-
changes you made
to X?

Z

Let's do the numbers!
"Care, community, comfort"
Dollar value?
Wrong letter, wrong (   ).
Offshore dummy corporations,
ancient, ex-
patriot,

ex-
change rates, moving
with cash, suspicion,
American practice.
Paradise.

       cf Milton *PL* Book IV
Satan
Hell himself.
Gates?
Brand name angels.
Everything fell.

Z-1

But not in love.
This is the post-temporal, post-serial, post-
A B Cs. Meeters & greeters
not allowed to cross (   ).

Z-2

Some kind of rent relief.
No one thinks that will happen this year.
Music.

Z-3

Good Investment:
Bed, Bath, and (   ).

Z-4

Announce personal   hymn
to make a chapel
         against wholesale (   )
devolution
                  (   )
                    A cigarette burning down at high speed
But there are X thousand people inside that cigarette.
"Well what's it like?"
"Children." (   )
                              retail or retell

Z-5

More or
less.

Z-6

The ancient came with me it was nothing I loved him
4.2 miles a brief stretch in the car he could not speak.

R / E N D I N G S

Votes destined to again unearth
mirth in the fabric of the morsel. Please do not underline
design my speechless-
ness, not while I am still
ill in the cave's
nave, resisting normal urges
purges to get on with things
cling. I doubt
out of time
lines, despite the impromptu gathering with ripe pears and cheese
ease. I imagine the clocks
rock, that the remainder is still
drill sweltering, water arcing
larking across the twilight
blight, the tourists
forest's crumbled immensity
density. Things continue to be planned ahead
dread but I no longer want to risk the materials, and so have taken
mistaken, fumbling, hoping for tact
fact to be productive, if not the detachment and humor we have come
dumb to expect.

"Awash" in the inscrutable palette of roses
roses unscented in the few
new perfection. Music rides
hides against honky-tonk beer
cheer. The moon

soon half full, never half empty. The second hand
lands outside the circle and
demand threatens to usurp the young road rats on the bus
us, all our distractions seem arbitrarily chosen like a form
norm of nostalgia in an indigo drawing: Whistler's fog. The heart's
art, caged in its gauze, making a poor sound. Gears slip and now
Dow it seems is being held up by so
low many cheats, instantly assembled, not one exactly like another,
others interchangeable. If a part hissed
mist, then it was hissing for good. Were we dangling, inevitably a delay
fade. Not anything I want, since delay's advent
meant sorrow. In truth, I have left, so
go little by little, it seems as if
life is a refutation. There is no one to comment or to abjure,
lure the little enlightened spots, herds
not words exactly, but what refuses to be underlined or condensed. One
sun steals the day, this for
more examples, the fog and the police car
star sitting above the browning grass and thought
wrought under the table. The cat is not dead but her eyes now wide
died with wonder. I think it must be wonder.

Everything quiet now in the zone
clone of retrieval. Through casts of zeal
real life narrows as a pipe carrying gray water to the zero gauge
age of reproduction in its video mirror
error's blind truce among those who still matter
latter loved, without courage, traced
faced with the fools of redemption who came easily out of the widow
ditto the indictment, ditto the harms

farms and the industrial park
dark collapse. Call this our time
I'm lonely for the integrity of sacred life, not religion, but love's
troves, its coil around sex
text comes after an ordeal of risk, the way we went back
lack or crisis because we had neglected the loom
room I suppose, even as the inventions are all for a violent solution
revolution, quiet as a street at dawn, in a city, a city so sadly
badly used.

POSTSCRIPT

And then these attenuated thistles.
Spoken from the sink, from the adamant.

There is no room, no
more room. Stuffed to the brink.

Object dispersed, whole into—
agitated, fielded. Throw us a flake.

Up to here. Up to the
mouth's bright contrast, its

sponsored aggressive silence, held
by interlocking dots.

Chapel among the drawings.
Trees up to their boughs in snow.

Or this brim, above the giddy mechanics
of instruments, their oiled

dissonant animation, the clock,
men with their staples

behind sliding doors in white hats,
the copper clad wall.

Taking these in
toward hibernating sorrow

things having been seen, persons
having drifted from view

pink repercussions of the metal,
a jacket, a cup.

Ann Lauterbach was born and grew up in New York City. After college (University of Wisconsin, Madison), she attended Columbia University on a Woodrow Wilson Fellowship, but moved to London before completing her MA in English literature. She lived in London for seven years, working variously in publishing and arts institutions. On her return, she worked for a number of years in art galleries in New York before she began teaching. She has taught at Brooklyn College, Columbia, Iowa, Princeton, and at the City College of New York and Graduate Center of CUNY. Since 1991 she has been Director of Writing in the Milton Avery School of the Arts at Bard College, where she has been, since 1999, Ruth and David Schwab II Professor of Languages and Literature. Lauterbach has received a number of awards and fellowships, including a Guggenheim Fellowship in 1986 and a John D. and Catherine T. MacArthur Fellowship in 1993. She lives in New York City and in Germantown, New York.

Penguin Poets

TED BERRIGAN
Selected Poems
The Sonnets

PHILIP BOOTH
Lifelines

JIM CARROLL
Fear of Dreaming
Void of Course

CARL DENNIS
New and Selected Poems
1974–2004
Practical Gods

BARBARA CULLY
Desire Reclining

DIANE DI PRIMA
Loba

STUART DISCHELL
Dig Safe

STEPHEN DOBYNS
Mystery, So Long
Pallbearers Envying the One
Who Rides
The Porcupine's Kisses

ROGER FANNING
Homesick

AMY GERSTLER
Crown of Weeds
Ghost Girl
Medicine
Nerve Storm

DEBORA GREGER
Desert Fathers, Uranium
Daughters
God
Western Art

ROBERT HUNTER
Sentinel

BARBARA JORDAN
Trace Elements

MARY KARR
Viper Rum

JACK KEROUAC
Book of Blues
Book of Haikus

JOANNE KYGER
As Ever

ANN LAUTERBACH
Hum
If in Time
On a Stair

PHYLLIS LEVIN
Mercury

WILLIAM LOGAN
Macbeth in Venice
Night Battle
Vain Empires

DEREK MAHON
Selected Poems

MICHAEL MCCLURE
Huge Dreams: San Francisco
and Beat Poems

CAROL MUSKE
An Octave Above Thunder

ALICE NOTLEY
The Descent of Alette
Disobedience
Mysteries of Small Houses

LAWRENCE RAAB
The Probable World
Visible Signs

PATTIANN ROGERS
Generations

STEPHANIE
   STRICKLAND
V

ANNE WALDMAN
Kill or Cure
Marriage: A Sentence
Structure of the World
   Compared to a Bubble

JAMES WELCH
Riding the Earthboy 40

PHILIP WHALEN
Overtime: Selected Poems

ROBERT WRIGLEY
Lives of the Animals
Reign of Snakes

JOHN YAU
Borrowed Love Poems